The Other Side of Longing

THE OTHER SIDE OF LONGING

Geraldine Mills   Lisa C. Taylor

ARLEN
HOUSE

The Other Side of Longing

is published in 2011 by
ARLEN HOUSE
an imprint of Arlen Publications Ltd
42 Grange Abbey Road
Baldoyle
Dublin 13
Ireland
Phone/Fax: 353 86 8207617
Email: arlenhouse@gmail.com

Distributed internationally by
SYRACUSE UNIVERSITY PRESS
621 Skytop Road, Suite 110
Syracuse, NY 13244–5290
Phone: 315–443–5534/Fax: 315–443–5545
Email: supress@syr.edu

ISBN 978–1–85132–014–1, paperback

© Geraldine Mills and Lisa C. Taylor, 2011

The moral rights of the authors have been asserted

Typesetting ¦ Arlen House
Printing ¦ Brunswick Press
Front Cover Image ¦ Russ Taylor

CONTENTS

INTRODUCTION

In January 2009, Lisa C. Taylor, Connecticut writer, received a Surdna Foundation Artist Fellowship to collaborate on a poetry collection with Galway writer Geraldine Mills. Lisa had become familiar with Geraldine's work when they met at the Cape Cod Writers' Conference in the summer of 2008. They began exchanging work via email in preparation for the collaboration in the summer of 2009 when Lisa arrived in Ireland. Working in a stone cottage in Carna, they crafted poems, took long walks, shared life stories, and forged a friendship. The Atlantic Ocean that both writers share became the central metaphor for their work.

After Lisa returned home, they continued to exchange poems and ideas via email and phone, revising and encouraging each other. In October of 2009, Geraldine travelled to Connecticut and Lisa organised readings at ACT: Arts at the Capitol Theater and at Eastern Connecticut State University where she teaches poetry and writing. Geraldine also visited classes and had a book signing at the University of Connecticut.

The work continued over the next ten months, with the authors exchanging information about their respective cultures and their lives, superstitions, traditions, folklore, flora and fauna. This resulting work represents two women who, whilst living on opposite sides of the Atlantic, share many commonalities.

THE OTHER SIDE OF LONGING

Geraldine Mills

THE CENTRE CANNOT HOLD

All night the wind has fought with our cottage.
It wakes and unnerves a part of me
that is unsettled by such noise,
as it is by all the colours of grey
we must live with throughout these summer days.

But your country has weather big enough for both of us.
It tumbles an outermost house into the sea
to career on a foreign beach in Chatham,
or a tornado whips up Dorothy into another state.
Hurricanes with names benign as dimpled grand-aunts
come to tea and scones,
but leave you stranded in their wake,
flood you with their grief.

A man once told me about the wind in Oklahoma.
It flung their screen door into Sam Weller's garden,
whipped one blade of straw from the barn
and drilled it right through the glass
of their kitchen window.
It held there, needle-straight, the pane intact,
lights blown, food in the icebox melting.

Before its contents folded onto the floor
they were allowed eat all at once;
pistachio, dark chocolate, black cherry,
while the straw lodged tight in its place,
breaking their mother's back.

Our lives are built on vagaries of weather,
one well-aimed gust and the sandbars
of memory crumble at our feet.

When the Time Comes

What of the mountain ablaze beyond our window?
Gorse, burning up the dark, so loud
we fear its crackle, hear its heat.

It spits out seeds that defy flame,
smuts of furze get washed into the stream's source
that tumbles down, picking up along the way:

whirligigs, caddis fly larvae, turf scent,
the luteus light of lesser celandine,
foxglove – that does the heart good just to look at.

It foams by the boundary of our land, so small,
yet there is nothing to stop it from thinking big –
from becoming ocean when the time comes.

Rushing under the bridge to a neighbour's field
down through bog tannin, it carries into the lake
before it takes itself to the river that flows

around the oarsmen, past the tea house at Menlo
under the Salmon Weir Bridge,
by the cathedral that still reels in the faithful.

It catches sight of the sea, boats by the Spanish Arch,
lets go of its name, heads out into the Atlantic, reaches
your coast with the memory of mountain, gorse, fire.

To Name it Twice

My hotel room comes with free drinks,
fruit, the baggage of its number – 911 –
and me looking out at skyscrapers,
a plane snailblazing the blue.

Down below is *iPod Touch* city-
life that can trip on the slip of a fingertip.
Traffic here is so slow it would never
catch on as a video game.

There's breakfast at Roxy's Deli
with towers of waffles, syrup.
Trick or Treat couples
are dancing at Suzy Woos.

Not the way I first saw this city, this city,
in the sixties with my sisters and our mother
at the top of the Empire State –
the tallest building even then,

as we squeezed into the swelter
of the recording booth
to sing damp and cold
out of ourselves; *Galway Bay*

dropping onto the black vinyl 78
that circled round and round.
It gathered each note into itself,
before it played us back,

our voices dancing across the rooftops,
over East River, Brooklyn, the Bronx;
above the skyline of Manhattan
where the blue held no fear of rain, no terror.

Cockshut

This word with such sharp teeth
for the hour between dog and wolf.
It slams itself closed like the gate
on the hens locked in for the night,
safe from the foxes that roam
with a longing to end-stop the breath
of a stray Rhode Island or Blue Silkie
caught between worlds,
when the sun is at the foot of the sky.

THE GREEN DRAGON IN GALWAY

Breathing the toil of sail on ocean,
the Race left Boston in fog.
Out beyond the feeding place of whales,
headed into storms that would pull bulls from chains.

They say Saint Brendan did the counter journey first,
launched from that Kerry creek with his blessed crew
long before Columbus stopped over in our town.
Stone chambers in Beaver Dam Hill attest to this,

found when a hurricane opened the story up again.
Monks that made America their home
and later our ancestors who left behind the famine
in hulls of boats. Never to return.

Now on this May morning – the sky still night,
the swans in the Claddagh Basin, their necks
folded into the underwing of sleep –
it comes out of the dark, the Green Dragon,

breathing flames of success to a homecoming,
seen from the Aran Islands and Black Head,
bonfires all along the coast, the headland
greeted at the winning gate by any hull worth its salt.

Waves of people heading towards the Docks,
cheers and drumming, fireworks on Nimmo's Pier,
even the swans are awake for this welcome
that would have made Columbus green.

THRESHOLD

Not having learned each other off by heart,
we tried to hammer out our differences
into the joists and floorboards
of our half-built house,
into the solid beams across our line of vision

when we lay in bed at night
to watch the dark fall through the space between,
the wind cursing in the cold hallway
ready to wake the kitchen with no hearth,
no spark among the clouds of ashes.

A threshold reached, I left through no door,
two chimneys punching holes in the sky,
black eyes of no windows looked after me
as I walked down no path
past the rows of potato drills
in our good neighbour's field.

The wind coming round the corner
slapped me in the face.
It didn't slow my step,
or the ropes of bindweed
choking the stones
all the way to the beach

where my footprints sank into sand
among the spindle toes of oystercatchers,
while gulls cried above the graveyard on the cliff,
mingling with god, with limpet shells.

SIDE-FOLD DRESS AT THE PEABODY MUSEUM

As if it were once mine, lost
and now found after years of searching.
As if I remember the woman tanning the skin first,
whether of elk or caribou I cannot recall.

Then stitching it with rows of porcupine quills
having won the sacred right to dye each piece,
moisten them in her mouth, flatten them,
burrow holes in the hide with an awl, thread them in.

Adding glass beads from Europe, brass buttons,
cowrie shells across the shoulder and little bunches
of red cloth sewn into it, dyed with madder,
all the way from somewhere near these shores,

used in the petticoats of women
from Conamara, Inis Mór, Boffin,
or as *swanskin* – that square of red flannel my mother
placed to my father's back when he couldn't work

from the pain meted out on building sites,
when life was a challenge of rattlesnake
around a bunch of arrows.

SONG FROM AN UNNAMED BOY
(Letterfrack Graveyard, 2009)

When I was a child I ate fire for breakfast,
the dark was a lantern-shaped star
I pulled on a string with the moon bright behind me
through the world with its windows ajar.

The clouds held onto the rain every morning,
the cows looked out to the edge of the sea,
until men told my father I only spelled trouble.
School was the place where my soul could run free.

That lie was a snake in the wall that was waiting.
When I rattled the loose stones, its venom fell out.
Bread that they baked held the sting of a scorpion,
eating their hypocrisy dressed up as devout.

My sorrow unmasked, they stamped on my laughter.
I was the lamb being dragged to the slaughter.

St Kevin Dreams He is a Mohegan

Here he can run faster than elk,
or the rabbit Brother Feichín
caught last night for supper,
and quahogs are far superior
to the penance of fish on Fridays,
so after sunrise and some corn grits
he dresses in his painted skins,
quiffs his hair with bison oil
and takes to Skunk Neck River,
his strong limbs full of grace,
the river with him,
blessed among the eyes that watch
from the Timothy Grass.

He kayaks to the trading post,
pays for a little indulgence
with his wampum
shaped and polished,
threaded on a string like rosary
to buy heavenly things for his missus,
blue beads and glittering trinkets,
that with a leap of faith
will offer him lordship of all he can survey.

In Search of Place

Quiet as it was said, I learned from birth
that we were not of place,
did not have the maps that charted lineage
buried around tribal walls.
We spoke in accents, not the Galway way,
or any other needed to mark us in.
Lived in a house where walls dripped
with the constant sound of lacking.

My mother lived for letters from New York
which promised greenbacks to wipe the slate clean.
Yet she the very one who sniffed and cried,
they were badly off to write in March,
their flights were booked for June.

Wallpaper cracks were patched up one more time,
good linen borrowed from a neighbour of that place.
Our faces pinned to the front window watched
for the first sound of Denny's car
from Shannon to bring them back again.

We rolled in the words they brought:
cookie, mall, faucet.
Faucet the one I never could translate,
no matter how I tried, for the rain barrel
was tapped to nothing but the sky.

I saw New York at eleven when my father died,
a man still out of place,
when aunts who needed to be kind
tried to ease small children's loss of him,
stretched out in the morgue, lips blue,
my little sister screaming when she kissed him cold.

Jackie Kennedy and my mother were widows together.
Photographs taken of her in that black dress
she wore all year and never touched again,
showed she looked more at home
on the steps of St. Patrick's Cathedral
than cycling the length of the hazel road
searching for some sign of him.

I could not wait to leave, holding my breath
until the train crossed the Shannon,
and I could sigh again in the smoggy,
faceless air of Gardiner Street.
Left behind the sharp taste of ripe nut,
wild strawberry foraged from out-of-way places,
to walk streets where being a stranger there came easy,
and my heart knew nothing of the way home.

SUMMER SOLSTICE

This is the contract between light and dark,
day and night.
Each accepts when the world belongs
to the other.
This is day's time, we know no sleep.
Swallows cutting
the sky are giddy with it.

Touched by the hand of Midas, everything
turns to gold:
common cat's-ear, bird's-foot trefoil,
buttercup.
The sun's monstrance gilds the high garden,
the cherry tree.
A prayer big enough to cover our best selves.

GET A LIFE, MR REMBRANDT!
(Artist self-portrait at the Wadsworth Atheneum)

Unwrinkle the brow, plump up the lips

Botox the furrow between the mournful eyes

Airbrush the weak chin from your father's side,
that swarthy nose from your mam's

Get the toilet-brush hair gelled

Flaunt diamond studs on the left lobe

A tattoo on the rippling biceps,
I luv u Hendrickje Stoffels

Put the grizzly bear coat up on eBay

Ditch the hat,
but don't let go of the hands

PARALLELS

I

Your stories I can enter
as if they were my own:
not the banshee keening from the underworld
but Granny Squannit of the Makiawisug
in her moccasins, her gnarled walnut skin,
who brought on storms.
When she took to the bed in her beehive chamber
with the whip-poor-will calling
and the wind tearing up trees all around,
who is to know whether
it was something unsavoury the bad spirits said,
or the English settlers that unravelled her.
Anyway, it took a medicine woman
one whole moon to bring her back to herself.

II

Leprechauns and the Makiawisug
are little people with big ideas –
gold-hoarders, earth-protectors.
Crocks of dreams at the end of arcs,
corn cakes in wicker at the edge of woods, glimmer.
One you must look straight in the eye
or he disappears on you,
the other considers such staring rude
and roots you to the spot
with no way of telling
how you might unglue yourself.

Kindness to them gives you largesse of corn,
quartz crystals, gifts they gather at night,
while our gold diggers in their glistening brogues

have a way of paying you back;
play games with money and promises,
fool you into thinking you have landed a prize
then mock you as it vanishes into thin air.

STANZABERRY
for Lisa and Russ

You bribed the leaves to hang on until I came
so I could read them in the way they shape you,
otherwise you would have to climb each tree,
stitch them back up there,
match each leaflet and lobe to its own.

But they clung on for me to see butter melt,
claret spill onto branches just above my head,
persimmon leaves flaunt their brilliance
all along the Fenton river, the Grist Mill,
Horse Barn Hill, where I heard Canada geese
spearhead their going in a startle of blue.

Here I learned the argument of squirrel
that tight-roped its way across the limb of tree,
malachite lichen on the house-side of trunk,
autumn rushing ahead of me on the road, while

each morning in the warm nest of my room
I woke to the New World
carrying dawn to my window
in a rose glow, blush, uplift of light
– a shrub you had no name for –
but I have crossed an ocean to see it,
so I call it giftberry, carnaberry, stanzaberry.

MOMIX AT THE JORGENSEN

Woman in a cage
sun dapples bright on water
dares to glide away

dragon divides
shadow moon in a red sky
emerges as man

white feathers of birds
bodies on a black stage lift
the arms of the sky

ribbons of light dance
limbs dabble in blue ether
sea anemones

crucible of wind
sidewinders, dreamcatchers flit
world returns itself

On Seeing your Photo of the Stone Chamber
for Charlie

To shape our childhood hideout
against a boundary wall, we hauled stones
across cleft and gryke of field.
With hands singing we dropped them into place.

The birds in the air looked down at us
like they would on some tribal people
rolling boulders across terrain to appease the gods,
sparks flying, the air singed with fire.

When we came back next morning to weave its roof
with hazel sticks and ferns, there was no trace of it,
as if something bigger than us came in the night,
picked it up and carried it across the sea

to Montville. The slope of the chamber's shadow
was hidden from the everyday, until an oak pulled
from its roots brought it back into the light,

the way fern curls green at its entrance.
Its stone, lintel, ivy – an opening so narrow
only a child's body could squeeze through,
birthing into the dark.

CONQUISTADORES

Docked on the table's oilcloth
like a ship at some foreign port,
the American parcel landed
to whoops of delight.

Our mother unhitched each cotton knot,
unfurled the sails of strong brown paper,
tore back the cardboard flaps,
letting all hands dive in, plunder.

Banners of lollipops and sweets,
Betty Crocker Muffin Mix
plaid pants, rainbow ribbons,
things we never dreamed of –

eyelash curlers, nail buffers,
'he-highls', 'standy-out slips'
so beautiful they made us believe
we could be someone else.

Dressed up in what we now became,
she frog-marched us across the floor,
our eyes full of stars,
our faces spangled with sugar,

the New World scent
conquering the kitchen,
more exotic than jasmine,
than spikenard.

When the Day's Work is Done

Like the priest at consecration
we raise our mobiles

high up to the window, believing
we will receive enough signal

so we can hear the voices of those
we are longing to hear from.

COMMON GROUND OF OCEAN

These things we have in common:
the year that we were born,
one son, one daughter, the love of a good man,
listening to Leonard Cohen when we were young
and listening to him still. The fish eye of blueberries,
the sacrament of words.

Each day we go to our chosen rooms
with themes from shared stories
picked up on our morning walks,
where the sea brands poems into rocks
and rabbits breed among the Lady's Bedstraw.

At lunch we eat like pilgrims from Lough Derg
or some such place where we deny ourselves
until the white page has done its holy work.
Pull our chairs to the foot of the fire
and warm ourselves more with conversation
than any heat the turf can give us back.

You tell me of men who spin yarn into afghans.
I answer with yarns that are spun out of piseogs,
let our unholy ghosts rise out of the smoke.
What would we call them if only we could name
the ones who have stolen our childhoods?

Scotty's Going Away Present

On leaving you gave me your collection of mustards:
Gulden's Diablo Hot, Annie's Bee Sting,
Mendocino seeds and suds, all the way from Fort Bragg,
a spicy beer mustard with red seal ale.

For years Nance Delmart's friends raved about hers,
so she began selling to stores in upstate New York.
Chile Sauce, Corn Relish and *Chicken Wing Sauce.*
You left me her unique zesty, *Sharp and Creamy.*

There was *Spice Brown* from Pittsburg,
even *Moutarde* prepared *a l'ancienne* from France.
Jalapeno came from Dan Jardine, head honcho of a ranch
off the interstate between Austin and San Antonio,

as well as one from Steel City Mustard Company.
Of course America's favourite *French's* was there
introduced at St Louis World Fair 1904
in its yellow breezy, squeezy bottle.

Zake's Fire Country had a secret ingredient, used
both for cooking and cleaning the family squirrel gun.
Whatever the case, scrumptious on meat and cheese,
as long as we didn't spill it on the good furniture.

The jar had a picture of Zake's farm in the fall of 1850,
kites flowing over clapboard barns, grain ripening,
mustard yellow trees, horses in the fields. For those
who liked it 'firey', Zake said. And you did.

Lisa C. Taylor

What I Will Bring

Three grey hummingbirds with an iridescent glint
on bee a-flutter wings. Good bread with caraway seeds
and a hint of cornmeal, tucked in next to a quote
by Eleanor Roosevelt,
'Do one thing every day that scares you'.

Down the road, violets dot the field with a centre
of twelve white blossoms, as if the purple had been
bleached away. Hyacinth like tiny grapes sprout
horizontal while forsythia shakes yellow stars
until they lie glitter-limp on the dirt.

Soon I will not be able to see the hill across the street
because hickory and sycamore trees will spread leaves
that transform the view into goldgreen hues
interrupted by triangles of light. A family of deer
nibble at the rhododendron, magenta scarves trailing
from narrow mouths.

I have followed the river for years, watched its leaping
in the springtime, receding in the fall. I carry the mood
of water within, like the piccolo chirp of frogs
and crickets. These are things I bring with me, to spread
out under shade trees, over mossy climbing rocks;
to lengthen our time.

PATIENCE AND THE SEA

I cannot see you
so I focus on six shades
of blue,
limpet shells,
gaudy scallop fans strewn
as if in travelling, they lost
their need for shelter.

It is never possible to keep another.

Like children squirming
past my grasp to find a language,
I can't preserve their laughter
nor feel your pain.

By a window facing west,
breakers change my point of view;
a fisherman's wife, fearing
news I cannot bear
until I see you striding over a hill,
basket of whiting
in your arms.

I bake no bread
but stack towels,
doubting each reunion.

In this way,
I hold you,
cast my lot
to sea.

THE OTHER SIDE OF LONGING

A place can get inside you
like a lover.
When you leave
to work or wed,
you're always trying
to get back there: the first clue

that you've fallen in love.

Salt is a foggy arm
you drape over exhaust smells,
and you greet morning
with *céad mile fáilte*.

You will tuck this place

into backpacks
and rolling carryon, speak
of it to passersby
who invite you for tea
or Guinness.

The romance of bougainvillea beckons
but still you yearn
for a tarnished sky
on that crooked beach
in a town whose name
doesn't matter.

That's how it is with love;
low clouds become endearing,
winds trap distance

on the other side of longing.

A GOOD AND TEMPORARY PLACE

I

We talked
by the shape of fire,
though none
can know another's life,
only arrange slices
with segments of orange
and lime shavings,
a good cabernet.
Here lavender curtsies,
blue tangle scaling stone.

II

Human sadness can't be rolled up,
its girth measured.
When we walk,
rabbits bound over hillocks
and the surface of water
is wrinkled as my mother's face.

III

In summer, sounds intensify;
my yard of katydid, tree frog,
cricket and owl. Connemara
with its murmuring wind,
not a single plane
though I've seen six graveyards,
all with shell offerings.

IV

By the bracken
I borrow smoky clouds
in rarified light,
gather blackberries for our porridge,
my fingers stained
with evidence.

V

And the wind cries
like a crazed fishwife
trying to sell the parts of hake
no one wants.
She's as mortal
as the cow in the field
and money can't save her,
doesn't matter a whit
in such a good
and temporary place.

BASKET OF YES

Down stone-rimmed paths
bordered by tufted purple vetch
and bindweed, braids of clouds
loosen in this kingdom of gull
and common hare.
The wind, full of opportunity,
whispers *here, here.*
I follow,
shadow of a graveyard
and death says, *why not?*
Turf-smoke exhales from chimneys,
while ancestors in cresting waves
leap like fruit
into a basket of welcome.

O summer of wild places,
gorse and sea spurge,
carve me a clearing
beyond the twin graves of child brothers,
let air creep through rock walls,
and a hand called *yes*
reach out
to help me over the gate.

SMALL SPARK
for Geraldine

Sometimes there's nothing to do
but open the shed
where you've stored
wood in neat stacks,
choose a log, properly dry.
But it sputters,
spits, and so you start again

at that place where turf and logs
tumble in concert, pick
a smaller, drier one,
your gloved hands carrying it
through windy rain to the cottage,
hair straw-wild across your forehead.
Waiting is the notebook
you will spread on your lap,
bright gills of ideas,
goat cheese on a rice cake,
curlicues of letters forming words

but the stove is coughing,
wants kindling
and you have none. Shoving
last week's news in its mouth,

it chokes forth a small spark
that you fan with your blank page
until the beginning of blaze
matures in front of you, chair,

words, heat turning together
like a salmon gliding
through the cold Atlantic,
trying to avoid
the line.

Take me to the cleft of paths
before the skerries and I will drop
down to the sea, alert
to the language of bogs,
ring forts interior dialogue.
I want to learn the origin
of remote outposts
where singing is speaking,
feasting is loving
and tales,
the work of decent folk.

When I reach beyond
my comma of houses,
differentiated by carved door,
white cat, paper wasps
under a defunct grill,
the hickory tree becomes important
for its history.

Carraig, loch, cashel,
women knitting sweaters
for men who won't return,
the parentheses of a cove,
upturn of rainspouts,
bracketed gates.

BOTH SIDES

A door opens in New England
while rain greens the fields
in Roundstone.

Over here

an island;
Nantucket or Cape Clear.

Walk toward a jetty,
study opalescent waves.

Wind exaggerates the leaves
of generous trees.

Red curtains, flapping linens,
curly-haired sheep.

Here – thickets and sleeping deer.
Peat fires, stone cottage, brown bread there.

Imagine steeples, watchmen, interstates.
Mine foxglove and bleeding hearts,
those swaggers of pink
on both sides of this border land,

these blousy waves.

HIDDEN DANGERS

An inky garter snake
with a fire stripe
coiled in road sand;
unearthliness driven
from Ireland by tenet
or myth. Last autumn
I heard the hollow clack
of rattler on the trail,
sprinted to asphalt.
Slithering unnerves me,
scrape of belly-walking
through forests, on quarries.
Now poison ivy skirts ferns
and I sidestep, alert
for skitter and hiss.

Once I spent an evening
in Kilkenny looking
for an apothecary, topical cream
for the poison rash but no one
understood till I said *insect bite.*

What lingers behind hillocks,
in mounds of peat? A whorl
of smoke stretches,
wraith cloud casting
this voyage
where loggerhead turtles
nest offshore,
bog-rosemary tangles grasses
and fists of plovers
press hieroglyphics
into the damp and stretching sand.

MATHEMATICS AND GEOGRAPHY

Sidestepping sheep droppings,
I hang clothes on the line
stretched taut
across a stone-rimmed meadow.
Nothing but hills of bell heather,
grazing cow and the pup
who greets me
in front of a red-doored cottage.
Porridge with six blueberries,
dear enough to ration,
and I'm not missing

four varieties of berry – buy one,
get two free, *to do* lists,
scarcity of hours.

A calf finds his mother,
nurses in the rain. Linen white
to her gold, she nudges him
with a broad nose
to another clearing,
new lushness.

Hours are tiny fingernails
tapping,
almost imperceptible,
quietly subtracting time.

SONNET TO CARNA

Stones and painted gates, sagging wind at sea,
either way I walk, the sky holds rain.
The grasses glisten treefrog, bitter gold
and yearning's pulsing star is night sky's stain.
Once I believed that joy was fear unmasked
but when ripe branches carry flower fire,
common moonlight seems tethered to a tree,
rock fragments are constrained by tangled briar.
Out in the field, the sheep await their death
and final sparrows fly on muted wings.
Chaos and derision dampen hills
and I forgo concern to lesser things.
The rain unmasks history, we are bound,
our stories tangled weed-like on the ground.

THE CHURCH OF THE SIX WINDS

In the night, the bleating goat wind
comes calling, plaintive cry
that seeps under the door until
the animal is at my bedside rubbing
his white horned head against my pillow
and I want to give him hay,
a promise and a ring.

I kneel praying to the longhaired woman
in the moors wind,
her dune-colored locks stirred up
like a lapwing beating
wings in a crazed tumble
through laden air.

Stranger rapping at the door wind
arrives in time for tea,
four short, one long;
windows answer with breathy sighs,
familiar moans.

This morning the wind
walks shoeless
on a stone wall, a tentative cry
leads me to unlock
the door, gather her
into my arms, make scones
with fresh cream and honey.

In the afternoon, the wind turns old,
full of rheumatism and rotting teeth,
a shallow exhalation
that takes unnaturally long.

Now wind is a sure lover,
hands all over me,
drawing breath in sharp little intakes.
I'm panting so hard,
I forget to hold onto my cap
and he takes it, holding it high
as I chase him down a path
rimmed with brambles,
collapse amid spurge and milkwort,
exhausted, reverent.

TRAINING MEMORY TO CHANGE HISTORY

What you see
when you look across the table:
my doubts about faith – intellect
posturing against soul. And does
it matter – the trappings in which
we find ourselves ensnared?

Still the same fears
about the world's emblems
of carnage and deprivation,
whether caring precludes action.

No matter which cluster of lilacs
I see from my window,
the sun will one day burn itself out,
an absolute like my mother's birth.
Carelessness doesn't slow

imminent morning nor distract
the clutch of night. We go forth
trusting that landscape
and culture matter.

Yesterday – rain's patina
on rooftops and roads;

now all I see
is all I will remember.

PLACE WITHOUT EDGES

There are three kinds
of hydrangea here:
concerto, ballad, faded sky.

O place without edges,
not a country or town
but a wildness where sheep
graze at will, stone walls unravel
and light sprints from gray
to aria
before the blue gate flaps shut.
Sun pinks clumps of grass,
a hip of beach belongs
to no one

and every verdant blossom
has a tufted double.

IRON LOCK

At the cockshut hour,
tips of heather uncovered
by a slice of blood moon,
he carries the last pail back,
washes calloused hands
with a cake of homemade soap.

Tomorrow he'll be awakened
by the braying of hungry children,
have spoons to lay out, fire to light
while the rhythm of bluster,
herd and harvest continues,
interrupted only by Sunday
when children are scrubbed
and piled into the station wagon,
Our Lady of Sorrows
for Mass, then a fragrant lamb stew
she has put to simmer
before dawn.

What does he ask himself
in the creaking hours
of darkness when wind
has a voice and ghost-limbs reach
through the keyhole?
Not new to divisions of land
nor death, he whispers *Mea Culpa*.
Grasses flatten, thresh
in the same breath
and he lies next to her,
hearing the iron lock of the gate
test its strength.

CRACK OF LIFE

There's a crack in everything.
That's how the life gets in – Leonard Cohen

Once I knew the hour
by tides and light, the sea speaking
in tongues
but I've forgotten the translation
of wildness.

Two hares cavort behind
a stone wall and berries ripen,
green nubs attracting color.
No mowing this expanse
the west wind ruffles.

I can't remember the name
of the fiery blossoms
that singe the hillside.

Standing still
as wind picks up,
my hair loosens
and I hear the bellow
of a far-off bull.
Rain stings like thistles;

then suddenly a slash
of blue.

MORNING WALK

An enviable view,
twenty-six windows, one door.
We pass by,
imagining residents.

A tern plays
the wind, slicing air
with a body built
to navigate freedom.

In my version,
he's a sharp-eyed businessman,
coiffed wife poring over romance novels
with titles like *Aching for Love*.
No children.
You agree about the children
but see domination
as a blight.

It's easy to have the finest house here,
a proclamation lost
on deserted roads.

Dipping into eddies
and flats like history,
we turn back,
pass the derelict famine house
with three chimneys,

both of us hungry,
the walk longer
and more treacherous
than we remembered.

PERSPECTIVE

The sky is an imposter,
world defined less
by what is
than what isn't. Down there,
a man

counts change in a biscuit tin.
His hands are rusting,
he doesn't know
whether to buy socks
or turf. The wheel
has not yet been invented,
house of sticks
covered in black plastic
but he isn't hungry,

can't remember the price of milk
or how to fry an egg.

It is dry inside his eyes.
His gloves lack fingers,
jacket without sleeves.

He remembers cotton sheets and duvets.
Somewhere a plate
of boiled potatoes.

A door closes,
windows scribbled with rain.
His left molar has a hole,
he can feel it with his tongue.
He tries to make a fist.

The weather unfolds,
stretching.
From up here,
it looks like
he is wilting.

INVISIBLE BOUNDARIES

This crescent body
we dip tentative toes into
as we once hip-hauled
children from our respective pasts
on holidays,
is a refuge.
It's a tenuous relationship,

necessary pairing
of humans and brine,
innards of salmon,
hollow lobster claws,
our feet touching
sand, rock, sea.

Oceans scatter shores,
parameters shifting with weather
and folly. A tsunami
is forced respect, puts religion
in front of us.
We can never outrun water
nor plumb its bottom.

In my sloop of imagining,
I navigate the boundary
in the middle of the Atlantic
where my territory ends,

yours begins.

MOVING LANDSCAPE

And you three to a bed
in a cold flat, remembering
Park Avenue, the Empire State Building,
children with shiny quarters
buying ice cream from a white truck.
I can see the older ones,
off to work, bringing home rashers
in a sack to flavor
soup for eleven. My father worked

long hours but there were only five
in a colonial house.
We had roast turkey with fixings
each November; different fears, rage.

A trick we both learned early;
to view life as the length of time
it takes a child to cross a field,
moving landscape of amber, olive,
transition marked with sparrows,
sleepy ferns, dandelions nodding
buttery heads. On a well-used chair

in a college lecture hall,
I studied the Renaissance, how to break away.
I had thought restlessness
was permanent, safety
something only others had
while across the Atlantic, you were
listening to Leonard Cohen,
making plans.

GERALDINE MILLS

A native of Galway, she is a poet and short fiction writer. Her poetry collections are *Unearthing your Own* (Bradshaw Books, 2001), *Toil the Dark Harvest* (Bradshaw Books, 2004) and *An Urgency of Stars* (Arlen House, 2009). Arlen House publishes her short fiction collections, *Lick of the Lizard* (2005) and *The Weight of Feathers* (2007) which are available internationally from Syracuse University Press, New York. *The Weight of Feathers* is taught at the University of Connecticut, while *Lick of the Lizard* is taught at Eastern Connecticut State University.

Winner of the millennium Hennessy/*Sunday Tribune* New Irish Writer Award, she was awarded an Arts Council Bursary in 2006 and, in 2007, a Patrick and Katherine Kavanagh Fellowship. In 2010, Geraldine was the inaugural winner of the RTÉ/Penguin Short Story Competition.

ACKNOWLEDGEMENTS

Versions of these poems first appeared in: *The Recorder: The Journal of the American Irish Historical Society*, *The Stony Thursday Book*, *Crannóg*, *Books Ireland*. Thanks to Máire Bradshaw for granting permission for 'In Search of Place'.

Buíochas ó chroí le Lisa C. Taylor.

A residency at Fundación Valparaiso in Spain enabled the editing of this collection to be completed.

The Arts Council and Culture Ireland, through bursaries and travel grants, have supported my career development, for which I am most grateful.

The Talking Stick Writers' Group and the Peer Group.

LISA C. TAYLOR

A longtime resident of New England, she is the author of two collections of poetry, *Falling Open* (Alpha Beat Press) and *Talking to Trees* (Finishing Line Press) which was nominated for the L.L. Winship PEN New England Award. Her poetry has been published in numerous literary journals including *Birmingham Poetry Review, Cape Rock, Crannóg, Midwest Poetry Review* and *Kimera*. Her work has appeared in the anthologies *Written with a Spoon: A Poet's Cookbook* (Sherman-Asher/Western Edge) and *The XY Files: Poems about the Male Experience* (Sherman-Asher/Western Edge). Lisa's poetry has been nominated for the Pushcart Prize. She received a Surdna Foundation Artist Fellowship in 2009 which enabled her to work on this collection with Geraldine Mills.

Lisa teaches Creative Writing at Eastern Connecticut State University and also works as a writer-in-residence in schools. She holds a Master of Fine Arts degree in Creative Writing from the Stonecoast Writers' Program at the University of Southern Maine. For more information see: www.lisactaylor.com or www.irelandpoetry.blogspot.com

ACKNOWLEDGEMENTS

Grateful acknowledgement is made to *Crannóg* magazine where the poem, 'Basket of Yes', first appeared.

The Surdna Foundation for providing this opportunity.

Still River Writers and the Enders Island Retreats.

Russ Taylor, first and best reader.

I owe a debt of gratitude to Geraldine Mills for her willingness to take on this project. Her humour, friendship, and knowledge have enriched my life.